Grief Journey

A Walk in the Shadow of Death

જ

Dennis Herschbach

To Marilyn,
God's peace,
Dennis Herschbach

Acknowledgements

⸱

There are a number of people who have been instrumental in the production of this book. It is with thanks that I acknowledge:

Linda Senta, my grief counselor, for reading my work, using it in her grief support groups, and encouraging me to put it in book form.

Ruth Wahlberg, who inspired me to keep writing and who encouraged me and gave me direction as a poet.

Linda Parks, who taught me the fundamentals of revision.

Kathie Denison, who read my work, encouraged me to find a publisher and then edited my manuscript.

My friends in Arrowhead Poets, who ministered to me when I needed new directions and who taught me.

Dedication

৵

This book is dedicated to the memory of my wife, Dorothy, a lovely person who, in general, cared for people, but most of all was devoted to family, especially her children and her grandchildren. She loved her husband with an undying devotion for forty years and seven months.

Dorothy had a special burden for young mothers, and as a WIC nurse and an MCH nurse influenced many. One young mother, after Dorothy's death, said Dorothy had saved her life.

On August 19, 2004, Dorothy was diagnosed with stage IV melanoma, it having gone undetected because of a rare presentation. Over the next year, the cancer progressed to the point it was no longer possible for her body to continue living, and she died August 1, 2005.

It is hoped that this writing will help others who grieve and that she will live on in its words for years to come.

A Walk in the Valley
of the Shadow of Death

ॐ

The Lord God has given me
the tongue of those who are taught,
that I may know how to sustain with a word
him that is weary.

Isaiah 50:4

It is said that everyone has a story to tell – this is *my* story, or more precisely, the story of my walk through the valley of the shadow of a death.

My wife, Dorothy, and I had been married for over thirty-nine years – thirty-nine years with few downs but just about always ups – when, on the evening of August 19, 2004, she received a phone call from a surgeon who had recently examined her. His words were devastating, and he informed her that she had stage four melanoma, a uniformly untreatable type of cancer.

At that moment, I knew *our* story was ending, and *my* story was beginning. Almost exactly a year later, Dorothy died. Our journey together was over, and my journey, now in the shadow of her death, became a forced march into an uncertain future.

Our story had been one of few storms, and most often, sunny days filled with joy, togetherness, comfort, peace – and most of all, a deep, undying love for each other.

My story of being in the valley of the shadow of death has been one of aloneness, sorrow, panic – and most of all, an ever-present grief. It is a story that is not over; now there *are* days when I see the sun; there *are* days when the valley is not quite so deep; there *are* days when the shadows are not quite so black. The brighter days have become more frequent as the journey has progressed, and now I observe others who are in earlier stages of grief than I am, walking the same route I was forced to take, and facing the same struggles I was forced to face.

And so, I invite you who grieve deeply, you who have reached the wider and sunnier valley, and you who wonder what the valley is like, to walk with me on a nearly two-year journey in the valley of the shadow of a loved one's death.

Through the poetry and the prose of one who has been there, feel the pain and the sorrow, identify feelings you may not know you have – but more importantly, walk with me as I experience the sun shining again, the valley getting less steep, and the shadow of a loved one's death beginning to dissipate.

There are no chapter breaks in this book; grief does not have chapter breaks, but is on a continuum. Not that it is a smooth upward curve out of the pit of despair. Instead, grief is a journey of progress, regression, plateaus and more progress, until you discover that you have come a long way, and are beginning to climb out of the valley of the shadow of the death of the loved one.

I had intended to continue writing until the second anniversary of Dorothy's death, but like all other aspects of my grieving, it was impossible to predict what the journey would be like, and so two months shy of two years, I know in my heart it is time to move on to other things. This does not mean my grieving is done – it may never be – but it means that my life has reached an equilibrium between my grief and life to live, and it is becoming more and more difficult to write poems about the grieving process.

And so, once again, I invite you, the reader, to walk my journey with me and gain a sense of how I reached the point where I live with the living and do not seek the dead among them.

* * * * * * *

Even though I walk through the
valley of the shadow of death,
I fear no evil;
for thou art with me;
thy rod and thy staff, they comfort me.

Psalm 23:4

Two, One, Alone

Two
A spirit raised in solitude
of pines and aspens, water, nature;
he learned habits of wildlife, secret places of the wood,
learned to meet circumstances: rain, sun, cold, warmth,
learned to love from those most close to him: family.
He, shy, withdrawn, insecure, fearful, a loner
seldom leaving forest, seldom passing a neat white house
near a highway, near a town so large, so cold.
He could not know the joy held behind its walls.

A spirit raised amid lives of others,
surrounded by friends, activities, people,
she learned the art of conversation, flirting, being feminine,
learned of acceptance: smiles, frowns, giving, taking,
learned to love by some unknown spirit need.
She, outgoing, welcoming companionship, needing touch,
living in a neat white house close to asphalt streets,
near a highway, near a town so small, so warm.
She could not know that joy passed near.

Two children, close, but worlds apart.
Two children, journeying in separate ways.
They grew through adolescence: he nineteen, she eighteen.
He, yet unsure, doubting self, living a "ta pocketa" dream life.
She, content with what she saw, full of joy, playful.
They lived, passing but not seeing,
meeting, unaware the other existed.
That one day eyes would open.
Are some things planned by God?

Two on convergent paths,
drawing nearer through the years until they meet at a locus;
slowly becoming less like two, more like one,
not knowing; then they see,
recognize that here is one who pleases,
has tenderness beyond anything imagined,
returns laughs, joy, love.
They give happiness.
Their lives, passing through each other, entwine –
two on the verge of melding into one.

One
They stand at the altar, still on two paths,
close enough to touch hands, to reach across the divide.
Soon their paths will merge, become one for them to tread.
In vows, they are one in spirit, sharing life.
All will not be roses; friction, uneven surfaces
scraped against each other, cry out, "STOP!"
Chafing wears away ridges, smoothes abrading interfaces
until they nest, comfortable in each other,
the divide gone.

Time, precious time, flits by unnoticed,
its passing absorbed by struggles to provide.
They walk one path: together, touching, loving, caring,
sharing life's wonders and dreams;
tomorrow we can, tomorrow we will;
family blesses, children to fill empty spaces – joy.
Fledglings leave nest, goodbyes said, tears shed;
one by one children become too old,
too restless to remain.

An empty nest, never empty hearts,
love which seemed to fill every space
grows even greater; their hearts could burst.

They walk to meet on a deserted road; at the sight of her,
his heart skips a beat as it had three decades before.
More years, the bond grows stronger; one is all that
can be seen by those who look; life is blessed.
Should they have so much when others have so little?
The end never imagined.

Happiness, contentment, joy, peace, love, health,
part of the process bringing them
to the beginning of what should be golden years.
Minor aches, pains, a twinge here, a twinge there, not concerned
about a small blip that can be fixed by modern medicine.
Routine physical. He meets her, hears the words, "It's cancer."
Words: Melanoma, stage four, no cure, sure death, clinical trial.
A small divide appears in the
single path between them – cancer.

Alone
Begins the battle with one end.
She will do anything to survive the dread.
He will support her every move, fill every need, hold her
when she wakes at night, covered with sweat of anxiety.
They pray, beseech their Lord for any hope, any sign of miracles.
Hope looms on the horizon: new drugs,
promising new procedures, tumor killing, positive.
And they fight on, day after day, consumed by the monster –
the divide grows wider.

A clinical trial; blew tumors
out of mice; answers to prayers.
Prophesy: "Thus sayeth the Lord." False hope: how cruel,
how merciless, how self-centered, how biased.
Advice: "Pray thus and so; she will be cured. Eat this, eat that,
surely healing powers placed within her will take over, cure."
They try, pray, beg for mercy, for more time, for a future to be.

And they fight on, day after day, consumed by the
monster; the divide grows wider.

Tests to which answers are already known –
are test needed to see evil well up?
The fight is over, nothing to do but wait for the day to come when
life passes; now, unbelievable strength for both. He to care;
she to live each day as though there will be one more.
Weariness of body, mind, and spirit overwhelms two lovers.
And they fight on, day after day, consumed by
the monster, and the divide grows wider.

They still hold hands, but the breach becomes
a barrier that isolates as they walk a changing path.
No more "tomorrow we can," no more "tomorrow we will."
Instead, realization there is no future for one;
soon will be only *alone*. The divide becomes wider day by day.
Time comes when the path they walk diverges far too swiftly.
Fingers barely touch as they reach for each other,
the expanse too broad for them to bridge.
She is gone. He is left standing.
Alone

November 5, 2005

During the first few months of Dorothy's illness, we clung to the hope that the ending to the story would be one of joy and thanksgiving, but it was not to be. Melanoma, it was revealed, is such a formidable foe that one doctor termed it "uniformly fatal." That told all.

I'll never understand how or why we did it, but we were able to live life as normally as possible, never dwelling on the obvious or on the tragedy of the moment. During those long months, however, I began to harbor some serious anger, not at God and most certainly not at my wife, but at the circumstances in which I knew I would surely be left. After her death, that anger boiled over in words.

Love was given so freely in our marriage that sacrifice had no definition. While she lived, everything, all giving, all sharing, all life had purpose; but when she died, the entire parameter of my life abruptly changed, and a new meaning had to evolve. Evolution takes time, and during the process many emotions had to surface, boil over, allowing the vitriol to evaporate.

It must be said, however, that even during these anger-filled times, if given the opportunity to do it all over again with no changes, the decision would be immediate. Of course! I who loved so deeply would do it all again in a heartbeat, simply because in her was life.

Lost Dreams

Eviscerate! The sound is ugly.
What could be worse than having one's heart torn from body,
    leaving an empty carcass gasping for meaning?
The heart can be given but retained,
    sacrificed yet continue beating.
We give, yield to love, and at the time the heart lives on;
    dreams, self, personal direction,
    sources of happiness are willingly sacrificed
    so the other may know fulfillment of dreams,
    can say on her deathbed,
"I have no regrets; I did all of which I dreamed."

But what of the other, when she is gone and time has passed
    for him to see needs, ambitions come to fruition;
    insides ripped out? *Eviscerated!*
He lives without a heart. Like a compass without a needle,
    it is there, but has no value: worn out, junk.
The void left where heart still beats is filled with anger:
    lost dreams, lost self, lost joy loom like hovering ghosts,
    reminders of what could have been; now will never be.
Can the heart be put in place, caused to beat once more?
    The timepiece cannot be turned back.
Lost dreams! *Eviscerated!*

November 21, 2005

The evolution of new meaning is not without pain. After forty years of marriage, to once again mark the box next to *single* on an application was no less than gut-wrenching. Every day, sometimes several times a day, sharp reminders of her being gone would stab at my soul, inflicting near-mortal wounds: simple things, like being at the mall, alone, for the first time.

At the Mall

Where IS she? It's been far too long!
One hour's gone by; I'm bored – they play a song.
It's canned, the kind that numbs the mind. I wait,
expecting to see her coming soon – late.
But then I know it's not to be.
She won't be here today; she's free.
I resolutely rise and leave.
Inside, I know I am alone. I grieve.

December 10, 2005

O f course one of the most difficult questions faced by those of us who grieve is, when do we clean out the closets and other storage areas that hold the things of our loved one's life? How long do we wait, what do we keep, what do we throw away, what do we give away?

All of these questions come at us like storm clouds during a time when we are hardly able to get up in the morning, let alone think logically. It is far more difficult than we have imagined. One by one the closets must be gone through; and just when we think that all of the heart-tearing discoveries have been made, it seems there is always one more drawer to be opened.

Boxing things up is difficult; placing them in the car is harder, but most difficult is leaving them at the collection center. I literally wanted to shout at the person receiving the boxes, "Do you have any idea what I am giving you? Do you even care?"

After the death of a loved one, especially someone with whom you have shared so many wonderful years, life changes direction in an instant. Everything becomes a decision of momentous proportions, even simple decisions such as where her sweaters should be given.

Emptying a Cedar Chest

A Pandora's Box filled with hope
sits idle, waiting to be opened;
inside, memories wrapped in love
and tissue paper,
wait to be released.

Lid opened,
white wedding dress once worn by her
leaps out; others follow: sweaters,
a receipt – "one diamond ring" –
and more.

Time to clear out those ghosts,
give to those who need.
Truth becomes reality;
she will not return.

I saved one, though;
maybe a granddaughter
will wear the gown some day.

December 15, 2005

Activities like boxing up clothing evoke tangible feelings, but there are hidden traps that hit us when we least expect them. The many times I called my oldest daughter "Dorothy" almost ripped my being in two, and even though I consciously told myself I would not do it again, I did. One of the most depressing feelings that I harbored was the constant urge to call home and tell my wife what was happening. For weeks I had the impulse to open my cell phone and dial our number; then I would realize it would be futile.

A Call

Yesterday –
the sunset awed.
I was there to see it.
I must call home.

Today –
a grandson was born.
I was there to hear his cry.
I must call home.

Tomorrow –
events will happen.
I'll be there to feel them.
I must call home.

Then, now, to come,
life goes on.
No reason to place that call;
she'll not answer.

December 29, 2005

The loss we experience encompasses all facets of our lives; and one by one the individual losses descend on us like unknown specters, circling about, but not really revealing themselves for what they are. Suddenly, one day, it dawns on us what is troubling our beings; and sometimes that realization is more painful than enlightening, because the true nature of our loss strikes and the cause of our pain is stripped bare.

We All Need

food for life,
water for slaking thirst,
friends for caring.

She fed my spirit,
watered my soul,
was my best friend.

I miss touch,
crave caress
from her hands.

January 2, 2006

At the end of March 2005, we were told that nothing had worked, and the tumors were totally out of control. By that time, they had invaded every part of her body, and we knew there was no going back. As we left the oncologist's office that day, I asked, "Well, what do you want to do?" and she said, "I want to go out for supper," and so we did. The days ahead were totally consumed with the finality of the situation, and Dorothy had far too much on her mind to even discuss. Finally, a week later, she asked me to call hospice.

For the next four months, she was at home, visited by a wonderfully compassionate nurse. But also during that time, she began to visibly fail, until, during the last two weeks of her life, she wanted to see no one and was confined to her bed.

She died at home, with me at her bedside. Death did not come easily, and the memory of that moment was emblazoned on my mind. For weeks afterward, her dying moments were all I could remember, to the exclusion of all other memories. In actuality, although the angst-causing memories of her last days lost their sharp edges after a few months, it was over a year before I could even consciously bring up memories of her being vibrant and full of life.

Lost Memories

In distant corners of my mind
lie memories that can't be found.
They must exist in there somewhere;
I know they're there.
Why can't I find them?

Near the front, newly made
memories refuse to fade.
For one year she suffered.
Why this remembrance? I don't know.

January 9, 2006

The death of a spouse brings forth emotions and thoughts that have never been experienced. We begin to think of scenarios that at one time would have only been termed bizarre, and new fears, new questions, and new ideas of life crowd our minds.

One of the ideas that hit me hard during this time had to do with my health. What if I needed a serious operation? What if I needed to have anesthesia and couldn't drive myself home? What if I became ill at home and had difficulty caring for myself? What if, what if, what if?

But the biggest what if – not a what if at all, because it will one day happen – was and still is: *who will be with me when I die?*

The Question

Who will be with me when I die?
I sat with her while she did.
I ask the question, and I sigh.

I watched and waited and I cried;
her soul from body slowly slid.
Who will be with me when I die?

I wonder, when death's close by,
to whom will I goodbye bid?
I ask the question, and I sigh.

When on my death bed I lie,
and from my eyes all light is hid,
who will be with me when I die?

I held her close, life gone awry.
Who'll hold me close as I did?
I ask the question, and I sigh.

The day will come when I will lie
beside death's door, farewell to bid.
Who will be with me when I die?
I ask the question, and I sigh.

January 12, 2006

By mid-January of that first year, Dorothy had been dead for five months. I was so proud that I had done everything the way it was supposed to have been done. I had showed people how to face death and get over it. I had grieved, I had cried, I was now ready to move on.

Because I had a year to think of being alone during Dorothy's illness, I had made plans for what I would do without her, and I had accomplished those plans, checking them off as if they were just a grocery list.

Feeling so confident that I was done grieving, I wrote the following words, knowing in my heart that I would be able to now put my world back in order.

Closed Door

Grief
walked through my door,
uninvited.

I met him head on,
pushed him out,
snapped the lock
behind.

Memories
will last a lifetime;
new fields call,
time to move on,
prepare a new slate;
be me.

I have much to give,
life to live;
past is past, door closed,
grief defeated.

January 15, 2006

I have never been so wrong in my entire life, thinking I had closed the door on one chapter of my life and thinking I was ready to move into a new chapter. Our minds have ways of protecting us and numbing us to grief and trauma that, if dumped on us in one heap, would surely destroy our being.

That is what my mind did; and little by little, my mind allowed the reality to seep through until sometime in late January of 2006, the floodgates opened, and all of my grief and all of my despair came rushing through the door I thought I had so tightly closed.

Life's events were the wedge that finally pried open the door to my grief that I had tried and wanted to seal shut forever. We had never celebrated New Year's Eve, but the first one without her brought pain that totally blindsided me. This was quickly followed by her birthday, what would have been our forty-first wedding anniversary, the death of a friend's son (I was asked to accompany the sheriff to their home when they were notified), and my conducting a funeral out of the same sanctuary in which Dorothy's funeral service had been held.

Life came to an almost total standstill while I grieved more deeply than I thought possible and I felt the genuine physical pain of a broken heart. With the help of a truly wonderful grief counselor, Linda, and regular attendance with a grief support group, I gradually came to an understanding of what had occurred: I had literally tried to close the door on Dorothy's death to avoid the pain and suffering accompanying grief.

In looking back, I realized I couldn't remember what I did during the months of August through January – it was as though they had never happened. All I knew was that, when the snow melted in April, one hundred tulips came up that I didn't re-member planting, and there was one huge pile of split firewood revealed where snowdrifts had been.

It was only then, months after her death, that I could even begin to put my life back together. If the reader will only look at the date of the previous poem and of the next, you will get the sense that something quite debilitating was going on during that time interval. It was during that time that the true extent of my loss was beginning to be realized, and I came to know that grieving is a long process, perhaps one that will never totally end.

Day after day, traps would spring up in the simple things I was doing, traps that would remind me of her and that she was no longer with me. One such time was a beautiful, sunny spring day.

Shadow on the Path

کے

The air is fresh
off the lake.
A smooth path,
walking is easy.
The sun is bright
on my back.

One shadow ...
there should be two.
They say she is with me in spirit,
in memory.
If this is true,
where is her shadow?

May 13, 2006

B ecause of what had happened in my life, my theology took a deep hit. When Dorothy was first diagnosed with cancer, I was sure that through prayer and modern medicine, she would be cured. Countless believers gathered around us, and prayer groups were organized for her. Acquaintances across the nation put her name on prayer lists, and I was positive that with all of that kind of prayer support and with the advances made in cancer treatment, we would surely have many years together.

I failed to take into account the nature of the beast. First, God rarely changes the laws of nature to meet our pleas, and second, there had been no new discoveries made in the treatment of melanoma in the last thirty years.

One evening, as I struggled with theological questions surrounding her death, I verbalized one to God. "Just what do you do up there, God?"

God at Work

What do you do up there, God?
You couldn't cure her,
not add one more day.
What do you do up there?

The pain of alone is too great,
hole in my soul too deep.
My being aches to hold her.
What do you do up there?

A friend called yesterday.
"Let's take a walk in the woods."
It lasted seven hours;
we talked of things past.

Another friend,
"I was sitting on my porch;
haven't talked in a long time."
We talked an hour.

A friend said,
"I care. Are you all right?"
I answered, "No."
We talked two hours.

What do you do up there, God?
You haven't removed my cross,
haven't made outcomes happy. ...
You love me through your people.

June 2, 2006

❧

By this time, I was beginning to see that being alone was not all a curse. Naturally I still missed Dorothy terribly, and I mourned her death every day. I mourned deeply, many times bursting into tears when a remembrance would wedge its way into my mind. But little by little, the layers of grief were being stripped away; little by little, I was learning that I could be alone, and at times aloneness could be a positive aspect of my life.

A Personal Wilderness

Alone in the wilderness,
I hear silence broken by sounds
of Whip-poor-wills
and nighttime buzzing
of six-legged creatures.

Alone in the silence,
I hear voices once lost amid
rumblings of sixteen-wheelers;
daytime hammerings of progress;
two-legged creatures too busy.

Alone in the wilderness of life,
I hear silence broken by sounds:
my own heart beating,
reverberations of my mind,
longings to have emptiness filled.

In the silence of alone,
I hear voices once lost
in conversation with sojourners;
voices lost in busyness of life.
In the silence of alone, I hear God.

June 6, 2006

Perhaps one of the benefits of being alone in my own personal wilderness was the opportunity to allow myself to fully, or at least as fully as possible, come to the awareness of the pain I was experiencing because of my great loss. One day I was struck with a most unusual thought, one that would place things in a better perspective for me. The idea was nothing that was profoundly earth-shattering; in fact, it had to be perfectly obvious to everyone – yet it took me months to realize. One of us had to die first, and because her pain was done and mine was only beginning, I suddenly realized I was thankful she would not have to suffer the grief I was feeling.

Gone First

Death is hard for the dying
and the one who cares.
Things too easily said,
"I'd trade places with you
on your death bed."
It cannot be.

When it is over,
one's set free.
The other –
the other! – must go on.
It is hard. As hard as dying?
Is it harder?

Then comes the thought,
"I'm thankful she died first."
She'll not suffer dying twice.

June 7, 2006

There would be stretches of time when I would be exceedingly busy, too busy, and I would have little time for doing things I most enjoyed. In retrospect, much of the busyness was self-inflicted and most likely an attempt to just fill time. I continued to do activities I had enjoyed before, but now the enjoyment was mostly gone; and at the end of the day I was sometimes left with the feeling I had been treading water, just barely keeping my head above the surface. Activities that had brought me great joy before now became time-fillers, even the activity of gardening.

A Fallow Garden

I had a garden where love was grown,
buds unfolded new each day,
each one unique in shape and form,
each blossom filled with hopes and dreams.

I have a garden where love has died.
The team of growers are no more,
one has left, one is behind.
Faith remains, small seeds scattered.

Some have seen a garden filled with joy.
Few have been there and returned.
One says, "It's a celebration.
Let me return to Paradise."

I know this garden in image only;
she waits near a golden throne.
I wait the day when we will meet;
walk a garden where love still grows.

July 10, 2006

$\backsim$

I had a vision of what our golden years would be like, and we were well on our way to fulfilling that vision. We loved each other as deeply, no, more deeply, than we ever had. As we walked, and we walked a great deal together, we held hands. When we rode in our car, we were almost always touching in some way. I envisioned us growing old together, aging at the same rate, sharing all that the years had to offer. But that was not to be. I mourn growing old alone.

Memories Do Not Age

Come, my love, grow old with me,
let lines of age a story be.
May silver threads our crowns adorn,
attest to all of lives well worn.

We'll walk together hand in hand,
perhaps go barefoot in the sand.
Young lovers' heads will turn to stare;
they'll wonder at the love we share.

At times you'll turn and look my way,
"I love you so" your eyes will say.
My eyes will cast the message back;
their love for you they will not lack.

My hair will gray, and steps will slow;
clear eyes will cloud, their age to show.
But you, my love, can never be
the one to say, "Grow old with me."

July 16, 2006

The summer of 2006 was the hottest on record; and by mid-July, the plants had lost the fresh greenness of spring, the soil had become arid, and physical activity was difficult because of the heat. I suppose this reflected my feelings as well, and I felt that life had become like the conditions provoked on nature by the weather: parched soil and drooping leaves.

Dog Days

Drab leaves droop under relentless rays,
illumination too intense for them to last.
Plants grope for drops of dew,
fibrous roots not nearly deep enough.
Birds perch silently in shaded cotes,
throats too parched to call.
Lakes that once were clear and blue,
now tepid, algae-brewing vats.
Life slows, overtaken by malaise.
Dog days of summer pass too slowly.

Drab lives droop from relentless grief,
memories too intense for a mind to bear.
Survivors grope for drops of peace,
faith not nearly deep enough.
Those left behind mourn silently,
souls too parched to speak.
Muted swans that once could laugh,
now tepid, bleakly brewing vats.
Life slows, overtaken by malaise.
Dog days of living pass too slowly.

August 2, 2006

I discovered a strange phenomenon: although each day passed so slowly, the weeks and months sped by as though someone had fast-forwarded my life. I have yet to find an explanation of why that would be, and I wonder which would be worse: to have the days speed by and the weeks drag on, or to have the weeks speed by and the days drag on.

One thing I did learn: while we are all different in the way we react to our grief, we are all the same. Almost everyone I have spoken to who is in my situation in life has a time of day that is more difficult than others. My "bad" time of day was always in the morning, shortly after I got up from my night's sleep. Some have a more difficult time in the evening, and others during meal times.

For me, time became a void to fill, but in doing so, time seemed to fly by.

It's All Relative

Days pass at a staggering pace.
   Minutes move single file.
      Seconds step slowly along.
From sunrise to sunset,
   time, a gulf too large to be
      filled by life, I feel.

Weeks speed by in a blinding blur
   measured by period events.
      Trash is collected on Friday.
He's here again, but can that be?
   Only yesterday the can was placed
      beside the curb and then returned, empty.

Months evaporate as a series of X's.
   Squares on a calendar blocked out.
      Soon leaves will drop, summer fade.
Pages turn in unending succession.
   Can autumn be here this soon?
      Spring flowers just bloomed, I thought.

Where did time go;
   what made it fly?
      Life's gone one year – or is it a week?
In a far distance I see
   nothing but the same.
      Will change come, I wonder.

August 8, 2006

Oને of the purposes I found for gardening was to grow fresh flowers to place on Dorothy's grave, and all summer long, whenever I had fresh flowers blooming, I would take a few stems to her gravesite and leave them. I didn't believe she knew I brought them, nor did I believe that in doing so I would in some way be connected to her spirit. Personally, I found comfort for myself in being reminded of what she had liked and feeling that I was doing something to keep her memory alive in me.

During these frequent visits, I was constantly meeting others who were performing the same ritual, or nearly the same. We would talk, reminisce, inquire about each other's state of being, and at times cry with each other. We belong to a club, and our membership is permanent.

The Club

Our club meets at random times,
always in the same place.
We walk; we talk.
Stories told by mute stones:
1966-2006, 1944-2005,
1956-1975, 1926-2004.
Each set of numbers a life cut short.

It's an exclusive club, only some allowed.
Dues are high; the price: a loved one's life.
Members share feelings; others nod in recognition.
Some come with flowers; others, tears,
both planted on hallowed ground.
We are survivors.

August 10, 2006

3

Some days are better than others with time of actual joy, while other days have waves of grief crashing down for no apparent reason other than Dorothy is no longer here as my wife and partner in life. By this time, the grief was not as raw and cutting as it had been at first, and most of the time the emotion tied to her death and the times of feeling my great loss were more like swells on the sea rather than breakers.

One day, I was on the breakwater of a harbor on Lake Superior. A stiff northeast wind was blowing, and I watched the waves strike the concrete wall – the first being relatively small, the second larger, the third larger still, and the fourth being large enough to cascade over the abutment. It dawned on me that this was what my grief had evolved to: periods of peace, followed by swells of pain.

Sea of Emotions

I walked today,
down by a Great Lake.
Wind burst from the northeast,
causing turmoil on calm water.
Waves beat on rocky shores,
following rhythms
small to large.

I lived today
in a world of grief.
Gusts of despair swept in,
sea waves spilled over my being,
fluid crests pummeled my soul,
formed no pattern,
each its own.

I learned today
as I walked along.
Waves become intermittent,
calm stretches longer between crashing swells.
Waters sometimes rest,
gentle waves
washing over.

August 26, 2006

How I longed to hold her one more time, to have her walk in the door and be able to greet her with a bear hug; to hear her say, "Hubby, I'm home." I'm sure I will want that for the remainder of my life, but I am not delusional, living in a fantasy world. I know it will never happen, and I know that I cannot dwell on impossible dreams. Yet, there are times that such thoughts slip into my mind, and I can only imagine what would happen if this dream came true.

One Day

If we could have one more day,
there'd not be time enough for all
the words that could be said.
I'd tell you of a grandson born,
read you words not written before,
tell of flowers new to my garden.

But words would take up too much time;
a long embrace would say it all.
I'd run my fingers through your hair;
caress your skin the way I would
when you were close enough to touch.
Still – there would be more to tell.

I miss you in everything I do;
day in, day out.
Simple things: fresh towels folded,
a morning cup of tea, a walk,
all done in loneliness, but for a memory.
I'd tell you of my loss.

I'd hold you close,
afraid to let you go
unless some force should once again us part.
I know you would, without my asking,
reach up to smooth unruly wisps of hair,
straighten my tie, hold my hand.

These are the things we'd do,
if we had one more day.

September 1, 2006

Sometimes I committed exceedingly foolish acts, acts that caused me pain even when I knew that pain was going to be the result. One such time occurred when I was finally looking through the contents of a small glass cabinet hanging on the bathroom wall. After thirteen months, I don't know what prompted me to look inside. Neither do I know what took me so long to open its doors; but that day in September, I was curious to find out what were its contents, and inside I found creams and soaps I had long forgotten. My eyes fell on a bottle in the back, her perfume, the kind she had worn almost all our married life, the kind I had given her when she had graduated from high school, three weeks after we had first met.

And then I did something so incredibly stupid; I can't believe I was so dumb. I sprayed the perfume on the sleeve of my shirt. What was I thinking? What did I think my reaction was going to be? Immediately, tears welled up in my eyes and then erupted into a flood as I sat on the floor and wept bitterly for several minutes. I could not wash the aroma from my sleeve or my skin, and for a day I was confronted with her vivid memory.

I know I will never spray that perfume again; but on the other hand, I strongly doubt if I will dispose of the bottle. It is beyond my capability to do either.

Essence of Her

There, hanging on the wall,
in a cabinet long ignored;
shelves stacked with memories in glass tombs.
One holds the Song of Wind,
essence of one who lived here long ago.

A hand moves against its will
to grasp the golden prize;
removes the plunger guard;
with one slight downward push,
charges the air with scent.

The room is filled with her;
painful reminder she is gone,
returning only in memory.
Tears flow unquenched in recognition.

Shelves will remain untouched
until the day
when there'll be no need for memories.
Two will share eternity
where again the Song of Wind will be.

September 4, 2006

It was over a year before I could begin remembering the innumerable happy moments we had shared during the more than thirty-nine years of marriage before cancer struck. Even then, the memories did not come rushing back in a torrent, but one by one. At first far and few between, they later began to surface in my conscious mind. I was alone, and much to my disbelief, I was getting quite accustomed to that situation, and the memories of her began to be a comfort rather than a cause for distress.

In the past, we had shared so much; and now in the present, although very differently, we still were able to share.

Without You

ॐ

Blue-sky days and starlit nights,
sunshine morn and sunset eves,
crystal lakes and northern lights,
flowers sweet and colored leaves;
those were the things we shared.

Fog-draped bluffs and sheltered lees,
quiet times and peaceful rests,
wood fires and iced teas,
goose down quilts and pillow sets;
those were the things we shared.

Memories and hours alone,
worlds apart and time to cope,
songs of love and graveside stone,
grace of God and eternal hope;
these are the things we share.

September 8, 2006

S ome people were wonderfully supportive, and it was beautiful how some people stood by me through all circumstances. One such person was Dorothy's sister, who called frequently and talked of small things. Never once did she call and ask, "How are you doing?" She knew how I was doing without asking, and so her phone visits were filled with pleasantries and tidbits of wit and information.

One day, when I was visiting her in person, she searched and found an old high school yearbook. It was from the year 1960 or so, I can't really remember the exact copy, but we sat and looked through the pages, reminiscing about this one or that one – and then I saw her picture, my wife-to-be, looking exactly like I remember her. Without thinking too much, I turned back to *my* picture and was blown away by what I saw.

Yearbook Pictures

A book was opened today;
I paused to look.
Page after page turned by,
each a series of rows and columns,
pictures neatly arranged.
The cover read *1960*.

She was there, caught in time,
a smile captured at just a right moment
to preserve her spirit:
bright, pert, filled with life.
Eyes revealed love's capability;
she could have had her choice.

I turned to another year,
one beyond hers, and looked again.
There was one out of synch:
nose too large to fit his face,
mouth too wide and eyes too narrow,
one not noticed in a crowd.

How could it be that she would see
any attracting feature in him?
Others thought the same.
She was true – for some reason.
I shouldn't ask why, only rejoice.
    I was the lucky one.

September 11, 2006

A utumn rolled around once again, when one of my joys had always been splitting and stacking firewood. Another joy in life was to hear the wild geese calling to each other as they would gather in preparation for their fall migration; and ever since I was a child, I felt some unknown pull from them as they flew overhead in their V formations. Perhaps their heading to warmer places signaled to me the end of another yearly cycle, and it happened again on this day.

Brothers of a Feather

A jay's sharp call,
thud of wood being split,
voices of geese gathering
to journey south.

I look up;
count until I reach eleven,
an odd number –
which one's mate is missing?

I cannot tell where she has gone;
she's missing as you fly on.
If you look down,
you will see only me.

Brother Goose, we do not fly solo;
we fly with others of our ilk,
resting in their wake. Yet –
oh kindred one, we fly alone.

September 16, 2006

The reminders of her were constant, and fortunately all were not so strong in their impact as to cause me to be moved to tears. As time went on, the reminders became more gentle – whether in their own nature or in my perception is debatable, I suppose. Yet, reminders were almost always present, and I had a difficult time discerning if I appreciated them or not. It seemed, in my case at any rate, that the beginning of my second year of life without Dorothy became less starkly tragic, but at the same time more confusing.

Mail Conundrum

The mailman came today;
placed in the box
magazines and letters, junk
addressed to me – and her.

I don't know what to think of that;
seeing her name invokes an inward scream.
"She's not here! Why don't you know?"
Mail separates into here and here not.

A feeling comes to bear
each time I read her name
as though she's still alive,
waiting for the mail to arrive.

I wish it would completely cease
to be delivered in this way.
I know that I will rue the day
not to see her name again.

September 18, 2006

I would get so tired of the same question, "How are you doing?" usually delivered with the same hang-dog look. Who knows how I am doing? I have no words to form an answer, and even if I do, you really don't want to take the time to listen, now do you? You want to hear, "Oh, the world is a wonderful place, all is well, and I'm glad she's not suffering anymore."

But that is not the case, so I answer, "I'm doing all right, some times better than others," and you go on to talk it over with another, to compare notes, to verify that you both observed the same reaction in me. You're satisfied.

Under Observation

꒜

A bug feels its way along
while those who watch
stand poised, looking glass in hand.
Which road will the thing take?
They scrutinize which way is chosen.
Will it fall into a huge sand trap
or go marching on?

Someone may take a poke – just a little –
observe how the critter will respond.
Like a gypsy with her crystal ball
reads the thing's reactions.
When they think they have it all,
conclusions can be found.
Sometimes I feel like that poor bug.

September 21, 2006

Perhaps you have been instructed by those who think they know what it is all about, and they have almost lectured you on the finer points of grieving. People said the dumbest things some times, like the lady who, when Dorothy had been dead for about five months, asked me, "Do you still miss her?" I answered politely, but choked back the words that had come to my lips.

Because I had heard so many myths about grieving and had believed them, when the first holiday came and went, I was rather shocked to find I felt no different. When three or four holidays had past, and I still felt as though I had made no progress, I realized that the calendar is immaterial. Turning a page, crossing off a day, starting a new year really makes no difference.

Then I started reading reality literature. I was impressed with the words of one of the world's great thinkers, C.S. Lewis, when, after his wife's death, he wrote, "One heals from an appendectomy. My leg is gone, and I shall always walk with a limp." Those who had been there professed that the second year of mourning was, in many ways, as difficult or more so than the first.

I was somewhat taken aback when at the one-year anniversary of Dorothy's death, my grief counselor told me, "I am really proud of you. You are working so hard at grieving," and then she added, "You're getting a really good start." I thought, *"Thank you very much!"*

Death to Clichés

~

Time heals all wounds and hurts.
You will get over it in time.
There will be someone else just right.
When the first Christmas comes and goes,
        then you will be better;
or her birthday, your wedding anniversary,
        perhaps it will be the new year.
Certainly by *one* year you'll be ready to move on.

Words of wisdom spoken by sages not yet there,
but those who have experience,
from high scholar to lowly drone,
bear messages far different
from the wisest of the rest.

Thanksgiving came and went,
and still the wound bled red.
Then came Christmas;
it wasn't what they'd said.
New Year's Day, a birthday,
an anniversary went by;
I knew that when the first year came
it would be no different.

The really wise ones,
those who've walked the mile before,
will say the second year
may be as relentless in its bore.
Don't be pushed or pulled,
grieve as your grieving needs.
Don't be afraid; you'll pass the test.

September 23, 2006

More than a year passed, and I still hadn't dreamed of her. I couldn't understand why, because I longed for some sense of her being with me. Others I spoke to who were in the same situation as I, would tell me of feelings of their loved one's presence, or of seeing signs such as a squirrel, a deer, or even an eagle. I would have been overjoyed with a dream about her.

Then one night, I did dream, and it was as perfect as could have been imagined. No words were spoken, only eye contact shared. Nothing was out of place, and she was the image of what I remembered seeing when we were twenty years old. I was left with a short time of contentment because of what I had been given.

The strange thing about dreams, though, is the realization that we cannot force them to occur. They come to us unexpectedly and vanish all too soon, leaving us wishing we could somehow call them back.

Night Vision

I dreamed of her last night. Atop the stair,
she turned and looked at me; I saw her
      beautiful as the first time,
hair perfect, not one strand misplaced,
      held back from 'round her face.
Her skin, her skin as fair as that day.
She smiled, looked away, to not look back.

Waves of joy washed over me.
I gently woke,
      knowing it was a dream, wishing for reality.
Then, overwhelming thankfulness
for a moment of reunion.
I lay, basking in her peace and love.
She'd entered my life; filled it again.

Days passed since she appeared so real to me;
      I gloried in the image.
Perhaps the time will come,
      she will look at me and smile.
Could I will it, she'd be here.
Oh, to never wake, an image preserved.

October 5, 2006

It has been over one year since Dorothy died, a year and two months to be more exact, and still moments of fear, almost panic, hit me. There is no way to know what will trigger this emotion, and stimuli come from all directions and at odd times, leaving me spinning and turning to meet the threat head-on.

It snowed yesterday, the first sign of approaching winter, and I immediately reacted, not overtly but inwardly, becoming agitated that the norm had been disrupted. I find the change of seasons to be the most discomforting, and this snowfall was far too early for its amount and intensity. Perhaps spring will be less intense, but then again, perhaps not.

Unexpected Change

Snow came early this year,
brought with it melancholy,
covered me with reality:
time passes too quickly.

The onset of a second winter
not anticipated with joy;
a white blanket of solitude
devoid of warmth and love.

Warm evenings have given way
to early darkness, long nights;
memories of winters past as blank
as new, smooth snow.
What did I do? I don't remember.

Fear grips my soul.
Will I fill long, dark hours
that come with winter?
Snow came early this year.

October 13, 2006

E arly on, I thought that this would be a far easier journey than it became, and I was rather cocksure of myself, believing that I would show the world how to grieve properly and then move on. Months later, the true grief hit with a force beyond which I could never have imagined; and it took months for me to work through feelings so much like fear and desperation that attacked my very spirit.

Only after I had grappled with the raw emotions accom-panying my being alone, could I begin to see the wisdom in the poem I had written back in February 2006. New water does fill the wake of the one who passed, but it doesn't happen spontaneously. I learned that it has to be searched for and found; and when you find it, you might be surprised at the form it takes. That is why it is important to become a member of society again, albeit in a different way. I found the importance of exploring many different avenues, some leading to dead ends, others to new and fruitful endeavors.

Canoeing as in Life

It lay ahead like a glassy sheet,
not one dimple upon its surface,
an expanse smooth as a table top,
polished, without a ripple.

Then came a knife to cut the calm,
absolute peace severed,
a sharp prow sliced through unity,
peeled back a wake, disrupted all.

Waves washed outward, disrupted, parted,
broke calm, shattered joy.
Life's paths are not traveled without
turmoil and destruction.

In the aftermath of chaos
breaking watery tranquility,
lake scar heals when new water
fills the void left by one who passed.

February 2006

Comfortable memories take many forms; and as insignificant as they may seem to others, some landmarks cradle cherished memories. One such place for me was the old Holiday Inn at a place called Canal Park. This had been the destination on our wedding night; and every time I passed that place, even when the name was changed, the memory of our first night together was wonderful in my mind. And after Dorothy died, when I had occasion to go to Canal Park, I would hold tight to the bitter-sweet memory it would invoke.

One day, when I had been to the antique shop on Canal Street, I looked, blinked, and looked again. My touchstone to the past was being razed. In fact, all that remained was the view of the lake, and a sudden sense of loss swept over me. On the drive home, I choked back tears of regret for what would be missing the next time I drove there, and I wondered how long it would be before all memory-provoking things of the past would be gone.

Demolition of a Memory

He remembers standing at the altar,
     saying "I do," eating turkey salad
     and white cake.
He remembers the snow-studded drive,
     checking in at midnight,
     opening a bottle of champagne.
He remembers the first night together,
     room service meals,
     a day too cold to leave the room.

Each time he drives by that place,
     its presence causes him to remember
     the start of a lifetime together.
Each time he is given
     a touchstone to hold tight,
     a place to which he can return.
And return he does – often.

He sees the wrecking ball swing,
     taking with it walls and windows,
     balconies and memories.
He drives past,
     passenger seat empty for a year;
     another hole is pierced.
He mourns – just a little – to have seen
     the demolition of a memory.

October 18, 2006

I was in shock for six months after Dorothy died, though I thought I was doing extremely well. I was so proud of myself. I was showing my family, my friends, my congregation how a person of faith ought to grieve. But then one day I woke up, and things were not all right. The shock wore off like Novocain after a dental procedure. The only problem: I had no pain killers to take, only buckets of tears to shed over my loss as the realization that she really was gone and not coming back hit me full force.

It was a fearful time, feeling like I was so totally alone in the world, and I wondered if this was the way life would end. There was no relief; and even with friends, in a crowd, in church, I had the acute feeling of being alone. This was a terribly painful time, real pain as in physical pain; my loss was that great.

One day, months after her death, I woke up. The sun was shining, and I actually felt like getting out of bed and doing something. What caused that transformation, I don't know, but it was welcome.

I still miss her more than these words can express, but I have found that even though I will always have a hole in my very being, I know I will live and be productive, and that is good.

Progress

Early grief is an open wound,
bleeding out emotions until
shock sets in, protecting
living from total death.
If not for routine, total shutdown
would bind up those who grieve:
brain locks into auto-pilot,
actions just reflexive.

Like an amputee, once sedation has worn off,
pain pierces through strong defense,
quickly building to a flood.
How much like fear is loneliness,
mimicking real, excruciating pain.
Will relief from nothingness come?
Where is the anesthetic?
Will I survive?

Day comes when alone is bearable,
even a blessing – it is then that I think of her.
Clear thoughts come easily in silence.
Oh, grief abounds, never to cease,
but new insights emerge. *"I will survive."*
We who grieve learn hard lessons.
We learn to live with alone, but not totally;
we have our memories of better days.

October 19, 2006

∽

Many times at weddings, I heard the preacher speak of the unity of two, and that in marriage there is a union into one flesh. It sounded good. I also was intrigued by the idea that when man marries, he is restored to a wholeness that had been separated from him when woman was formed. You know the story: God took a rib from Adam and made Eve. I always thought that this idea of marriage, healing the separation, was very romantic and a good story.

However, when Dorothy died, and as time went by, I began to realize, at least in my own case, that what the writer of Genesis had said was absolutely true. No matter where I went or what I did, I always felt as though I was not complete. I have no other explanation than to say that the account in Genesis is not mere words, but a lasting truth about humanity.

One Flesh

⁓

Words are cheap,
or so the saying goes.
Some know the truth
about spoken words:
promises and vows.

An ancient knew their force,
penned the thought,
"And two shall become one flesh."
It is a mystery yet today,
how two words, "I do,"
create unity from separateness.

There are struggles in the union
of man and woman into one.
Time passes; new bodies
don't seem all that different
from what had been.

Little thought is given
to the fact that it cannot
go on forever; one must leave first.
It is when one half is excised
from the single being that
knowledge becomes abundant.

Only when she is missing
does reality strike with full force.
Their lives were truly one,
now he must go on
with a part missing.
He limps through life, an amputee.

October 21, 2006

Quite some time ago, a pastor friend of mine said that, in his experience dealing with grieving spouses, it takes at least two full cycles, two years, before the intense grief begins to subside and the griever can find a more lasting peace. I didn't want to believe him. After all, I was stronger than that, able to leap grief with a single bound, getting over it faster than a speeding bullet, a man built of steel. Now I knew what it was like to be a piece of crumbling talc.

Unfortunately, he was right. The days pass by, but with difficulty, and the evenings are a blessed relief, because I know it is soon bedtime. And all around me are familiar things to do that are not familiar anymore. They are the same, but life is different, and I keep looking for the sameness, knowing full well that sameness will never be again.

An Empty Window

She would stand at a window,
      the one looking out back,
      over the yard and beyond.
When I would be working,
      walking from place to place,
      she would be there, eyes following me.
In the fall, before winter,
      I'd see her inside,
      safe from the cold, while I'd be out,
      tucking plants to bed for the long nights.
I would catch her watching me; sometimes
      she would do things no one else would see
      to make me laugh.

Today I spent the hours transplanting
      antique roses, curling up hoses,
      splitting firewood, topping off the compost heap.
I walked by that window,
      going from here to there and there to here,
      more than once, each time looking up.
      She wasn't there.
Then, there was purpose for all I did;
      now I do for doing's sake
      that which must be done.
I did look one more time – just in case.
She wasn't there. I didn't laugh.

October 23, 2006

One of Dorothy's greatest regrets was knowing that she would not be able to see her grandbabies, as she called them, grow up. Not only that, she rued the fact that some of them would forget her, and some would be born after she died. Because I knew how much it pained her to leave them, I had more than a little remorse, when in March 2006, I learned that my younger daughter was going to have another baby.

But as the days and weeks and months went by, I became more and more aware of the feeling of Dorothy's presence surrounding the pregnancy. Please do not be mistaken by my words: there was no ghost, no spirit swirling around, but the memory of how much she loved those babies became more and more vivid.

Then one day a lady who had been a dear friend of Dorothy told me of a dream she had. Once again, I didn't see this as a mystical way of Dorothy communicating with us, but the image was beautiful. She dreamed that Dorothy was sitting on a porch, rocking in a chair, and she picked up a newborn, hugged it, and said, *"This is the best one yet."*

On this day, November 1, 2006, I went to see my just-born grandson, and it was as if I heard her voice, though there was no sound. Somehow I know I did, and it was beautiful.

Rejoice when you have memories that seem so real. They don't happen often, at least not to me, so savor them when they do.

Present Always

A child was born this morn,
a boy, healthy as one should be.
He was part her and part me,
his mother more so.

In the early hours I was there,
saw his newborn face, his hair,
and heard her voice, clearly:
"Look what you did!"

Six times before I heard those words,
high praise to any daughter's ear,
more so from her to them.
She was revered, now missed.

Did any other hear those words,
mine the only senses keen to her presence?
Or were there others?
She loved those babies more than life.

Was she there in ways not understood?
We mortal beings can be too unknowing.
Hear that? Words of joy:
"This is the best one yet."

November 1, 2006

M emories are precious commodities that are sometimes difficult to come by. Strange as it may seem, in the weeks and
months following Dorothy's death, it took extreme concentration
to bring up any memories that were positive, let alone happy, and I
wondered if I had forever lost those things I wanted to remember.

Now, some fifteen months after her death, I began to experience
lovely memories once again, memories that were so vivid that it
seemed she could materialize at any moment. At times this brought
tears, but even amid the tears was a joy in knowing that I had not
forgotten.

But now, along with the wonderful memories that began to spontaneously well up, came the apprehension that in time I would forget,
and the memories would no longer be manifest. I resented anything
or anybody that diluted the memory of her, and at times simply
wanted to place myself in situations that demanded I remember.

Then came the realization – I don't know how or what prompted
it – that I would *not* forget, and there would always be triggers that
would jog my mind and preserve memories forever.

Measuring Forever

How long is a memory?
Does it last an inch,
      or could it be a mile?
Can it fill a quart,
      overflow a barrel?

Some things make no sense.

I fear losing her memory,
      abhor that which diminishes.
Can a remembrance grow,
      become more vivid with time?
How is clarity preserved?

Days, weeks, months come and go,
      splashed with sights and sounds,
      reminding me that who once was
            exists no more.
A promise kept; I'll not forget.

Cherished memories have no bounds.

November 4, 2006

M onths ago, someone told me that pleasant memories would return, and I scoffed. It was impossible for me to conceive of good memories returning when all I could remember was sickness and death, but the person who shared that wisdom with me had been down this road already. Much to my amazement there came a time – it sneaked in when I wasn't looking – when I was reliving good times.

Then I couldn't shut off the flood, and it seemed that each day new and vibrant memories would spring into my mind, uninvited but welcome. Memories come as bittersweet potion: bitter because they bring sadness for what has been lost; sweet because they bring joy in knowing what we had.

I now can rest, knowing that memories will continue to be a part of my being, and they will not go away. But they will always bring with them some melancholy.

Forty Years Ago Today

꒜

The column header read *BYGONES*,
in bold print, **November 7, 1966**,
followed by accounts of happenings
forty years past – important news.
Missing was one item.

We walked that day,
along a frozen river, carefully.
She carried more weight,
thirty pounds if I remember,
not too nimble with just cause.
It was almost time, or so we thought.

[Our daughter turns forty, three days from now.]

BYGONES is meant to jog a memory.
It did it well.
Behind closed eyes I saw ice-rimmed rocks,
heard rippling water spill over drops,
felt her hand in mine.
She couldn't slip.

I returned to that moment, almost real,
when we were young and life was good.
To hold a memory in one's heart
is more sought than any riches.
Pain comes knowing the past is over,
written forever in a place called bygones.

November 7, 2006

For almost ten years I have served as pastor in a small Lutheran Church on the north shore of Lake Superior in a community with the quaint name, Castle Danger. It is a small congregation, housed in the quintessential white, country church. We loved that church, I still do, and each Sunday she would drive me to service so that I could relax and prepare my mind for the job ahead.

The joy I would get from seeing her – she always sat in the front, smiling at me and showing me her approval – was beyond explanation. How can one explain the swelling of pride and joy in one's chest? It cannot be put into words.

Whenever our small choir would sing, I was the only bass, and she would always tell me how much she loved to hear my voice, and that she could easily pick it out from the others.

I still preach, and I still sing, but now there is no one to tell me that my sermon wasn't the best she had heard me deliver, or that she could listen to me forever. Things will never be the same.

Preaching to an Empty Pew

I look out from my perch,
some call it a pulpit,
see faces upturned,
expectant, waiting for the Word.
I deliver;
something is missing.

There in the front, to the left,
is where she would sit,
never missing a Sunday,
singing to the Lord,
a little off-key.

Now that spot is occupied by another,
not empty –
though to me it is.
She was my critic,
my rock to keep me grounded,
one who was honest.

Sometimes when I'm alone,
I sit in that spot,
study sunlight on stained glass,
wish she was here.
Then I leave.

November 15, 2006

As much as we wish it were not so, change is inevitable, coming at us whether we do anything or not. When our spouse dies, we are forced to change, and this change is so abrupt that for a time, we flounder as surely as if we had fallen overboard at sea and were abandoned. We are left in a sea of uncertainty to find answers to life's most difficult questions: *Who am I? What will I do? How will this end? Will it end?*

The changes thrust upon us cause unrest to our souls, and we must change, because change will take place with or without us. Change demands change. It surges ahead, heedless of the crushed lives it leaves in its wake, and so we might as well take the helm of our life and make some effort to plot our own course. It is difficult, and requires a great deal of energy; but we can force ourselves to move, to take action, to look for purpose, even though at times purpose might be almost impossible to find.

The world will not come to us who grieve. Certainly, for a short time, people gather around; but soon they are back to their own worlds, busy, with purpose and full of activity. Unfortunately, we who are alone do not fit in well with their worlds. Seldom do people drop in to visit; seldom do they invite the lone one to join their group. It is not intentional; it just happens.

Often people would meet me in the store or on the street, and I'd hear, "I think of you so often," and I would want to say, "If you think of me, why don't you call or stop over? You know I can't hear your thoughts, see your thoughts, feel your thoughts."

I did find, however, that if I initiated a visit, an activity, any kind of get-together, people were glad, or at least seemed to be, to have me around. There were things to do, groups to join, activities to enjoy, but *I* had to take the initiative.

On a personal note, here are some things I did: wrote poetry, joined the League of Minnesota Poets, went to baseball games, gardened, went on a mission trip to Honduras, hiked, kept the bird feeders full. To do any one of these took energy. I wanted to just sit; but when I forced myself up off the couch and did something, I felt better. Someone told me that when one loses a spouse, they must "re-member" – that is, become a member of society again, but in a different way. That person was right.

Try to Re-member

I remember when
couples came to visit,
sometimes in cliques;
men in one room, women another,
sometimes all in one,
always even numbers.

Odd man out, they come no more.
No drop-in guests,
seldom requests to "join us."
They care, deeply, but life calls;
yet, there is that odd man out.

Who am I? I don't know.
Grieving is such hard work.
Why move, try, reach out?

Change happens without permission –
we only steer it.
Grab hold the tiller,
set a course, sail boldly
into uncharted waters
for no purpose other than to do –
but do.

Society is still there, it has not ceased.
Time comes to re-enter,
to meet fellow sojourners
on this trip called life,
to form a plan for re-joining the human race,
renew my membership in the fellowship of humankind.
I will remember, but I must re-member.

November 17, 2006

The term miracle is too easily bantered about, too frequently used to explain the unexplainable, but I don't know how else to explain our ability to live through great and devastating loss. What a marvelously magnificent thing is the human spirit. It can be trampled upon, bent and twisted, stretched to the breaking point, but it seldom does. This is not to say that the human spirit cannot be broken completely; it can, or at least in some cases it can almost come to that end.

But the spirit has a remarkable way of preserving itself. Since Dorothy's death, I have become acutely aware of just how resilient is the spirit, because I see sorrow through different lenses now. I see a husband whose lovely wife died, taking up his tools and creating furniture. I see a wife whose husband died, doing eldercare at a nursing home. All around me, even in my own life, I see the spirit gaining strength. I see people begin to live once more.

True, the life they live is different, and the loss is never forgotten, but neither does living cease. Life goes on, because the human spirit is far stronger than any of us imagined it could be.

Monuments to Strength

Great walls are made to stand
unbroken by pounding forces.
Battered by relentless blows,
it seems they would tumble down,
form piles of rubble
never to be resurrected.

Trees stand tall against all odds.
Like aged ones
bent to nearly breaking point
by unseen hands of gale winds,
they do not split.
Trunks snap upright, crowns held high
in strength and majesty;
missing branches,
resolve not broken.

The human spirit,
when pain of loss becomes so great
it seems to breach all defenses,
stands stronger than ever thought.
When sorrows bow it
to the breaking point, it doesn't splinter.
More strength than can be known
found by those bent low.

Walls, well built by hands, stand.
Trees, marvelously made, spring back.
Human spirit, resilient beyond thought, endures.

November 25, 2006

The process of grieving is difficult enough without having to go it alone, but all too frequently this is what happens. Family just doesn't always understand, and this leads to hurtful words, to feelings of abandonment, to thoughtlessness. There are times when family members would rather ignore the whole matter of grief, because they simply don't know how to deal with it, or our grief reminds them that their turn will eventually come when they will walk in our shoes. Friends also get on with their lives, and we who grieve are often left to grieve as best we can.

Where can we turn? Inside of us is a desire, the outright need, to tell our story. People constantly ask, "How are you doing?" For most, this is a question to which they really don't want to know the answer. They expect to hear, "Oh, I'm doing quite well," and they expect to see these words delivered with a smile. Others may truly care, but they don't have an hour to sit and listen; neither do I have the desire to sit and talk nonstop.

I found the answer in the form of a support group, where everyone participating had experienced the death of a loved one, some very recently, others some time ago. At each meeting, we were encouraged to tell our story, or at least a version of it, to the group, and then a topic would emerge. Soon, almost every person would be sharing feelings, some not even previously recognized, and we would realize we were not alone in our struggles. What a blessing that group was, and still is, to me.

Support

Stories must be told over and again
until there is no need to tell.
Who will listen for the hundredth time,
nod in agreement with understanding eyes?
Those who know.

Tuesday comes, first or third,
it doesn't matter.
THE GROUP meets that night;
some will be new, some old friends.
All have suffered loss.

We talk, tell our stories again,
feel each other's pain;
some weep, all share.
Many shoulders make burdens lighter.

December 1, 2006

The first Christmas without Dorothy was not as difficult as I had anticipated. I believe there were reasons for that, not the least of which was that the shock of being alone had not yet worn off. I was still being sheltered from the full blast of my loss, and my psyche was shielding me from being hit with more than I could withstand.

Secondly, my entire family was coming home, and the anticipation of that gathering occupied much of my thought and time. Knowing they would be home – children, grandchildren, in-laws – gave me incentive to decorate the house and put up a Christmas tree. That removed some of the sting.

And then, I was able to do something really special. I had given Dorothy a very nice diamond for our engagement, and over the years we had it set in a unique band of white and yellow gold. My conundrum was what to do with one ring, two daughters, and a daughter-in-law. I had decided before Dorothy died, and had shared the idea with her, that I would have her ring disassembled, add the missing components, and have three rings made, each identical, each having an unspecified part of Mom's ring in it. Each daughter would get Mom's ring. It was one delightful gift to give, and it seemed that I was giving to Dorothy, and not to someone else.

This year is different. The numbness has worn off, and I recognize my grief for what it is. Family will not be coming home this year for Christmas, and I have no special gift to give. This year, Christmas is not something I look forward to with anticipation, and I fear it will simply happen.

No One to Please

All around blare messages,
Christmas will be here.
Reminders fill papers,
airwaves – radio, TV:
"Don't forget that special someone."

Lovely faces reflect joy,
reveal surprise, delight and awe.
Diamonds, pearls, gold, silver;
gifts bestowed upon a queen,
once dreamed for mine.

Images of fireside trysts,
small packages secreted in,
presents presented at right times
garner looks of endearment,
warm embraces, kisses,
signs of love.

Christmas ads awaken memories
of past events never to be repeated.
A somewhat mended heart
tears open with each reminder
of what is wished.

December 5, 2006

In the months following Dorothy's death, everything I did was out of context and separated from the normal I had known for many years. Simple things such as going to church, attending a wedding, even eating at a restaurant, felt absolutely strange. I believe it is totally impossible to put into words what a surviving spouse experiences when normalcy in any sense of the word does not exist. The same can be said about the feelings after the loss of a child, a sibling, or a parent. Each of us comes from a dif-ferent set of circumstances, but all who have suffered the loss of a loved one have suffered the loss of normal. Like so many of life's experiences, only those who have walked the walk can know what great loss entails.

Then one day some sixteen months after her death, I went out for breakfast and never gave a thought to the fact I was alone. In fact, it didn't dawn on me until later in the day that what I had done was normal, a new normal for sure, but normal.

Normal Is As Normal Does

There's a place where breakfast is served:
pancakes, omelets, and more.
I arrive alone,
order two eggs, over easy;
two bacon strips, crisp;
three cakes, with syrup.
Washed down with coffee, it's good.
I read the paper,
pay the tab,
and leave – as normal.

Day passes;
I tell a friend;
reality unveils realization.
The meal satisfied –
nothing seemed out of place
good food to enjoy,
paper to peruse,
coffee to savor –
a new normal.

December 7, 2006

~~*~~

Dorothy and I were not very good dancers. She insisted on leading, and I had such poor coordination that we couldn't dance with anyone but each other. Together, though, we had developed our own steps and movements, and move together we did. Some said we were good – but we weren't. Sometimes we would dance around the house to hummed tunes; sometimes to no tunes at all.

One such moment occurred on a night after a fresh coating of snow had blanketed the ground. The full moon reflected off its purity with such brilliance that sharply defined shadows were formed outside, and the moonlight reflected through the window and illuminated our living room. It was on that night that we danced to the tune of cancer.

There would be other dances, but that one, in particular, remains a memory.

Moolight Dance

Moonlight floods new-fallen snow,
reflects through windows,
fills dark rooms with muted,
lunar radiance.
We gently sway to unplayed songs,
bodies nestled in comfort,
step for step matched
in time to love's slow cadence.

I sit and stare;
same moon showers earth
with new light,
radiance recognized,
but different.
We gently sway to a new song played,
spirit to spirit,
unfamiliar steps now danced
in time to an eternal beat.

December 10, 2006

Christmas at our house was filled with traditions; I suspect this is true with many families. Getting the tree was a greatly anticipated task, and each autumn we would trudge the forest together, looking for just the right tree. Then we would mark it with a colored ribbon so it could be easily found in December, even if the tree were covered with snow. Come time, I'd cut it down, and we'd drag it home.

Tree-trimming day was an elaborate affair. Christmas carols would be played, and the rich voice of Johnny Mathis would fill the rooms. I would attach the tree stand and make sure the tree stood vertically; then I would string the lights. That was my part. I would sit back and watch my family place each ornament on just the right branch. Dorothy always created a theme, whether it was bird nests, angels, snowmen, or whatever.

When the kids' bedtimes had come and gone and we were alone, we would sit in the room, darkened except for the tree lights, and hold each other and stare. Invariably, one of us would eventually say, "You know, I think this is the best tree we've ever had."

This, the second year of decorating the tree alone, I had planned what I was going to do. I would put up the tree, decorate it as best I could, pour myself a LARGE glass of wine, sit on the couch, look at the tree, and weep gallons of tears. I just knew that was what I'd do.

Surprised by Peace

Fresh from the forest, evergreen odors
stand in a corner
waiting to be adorned
according to season's tune.

Memories hung on a tree:
glass balls from Italy,
colored cones from generations past,
bubble lights and shiny baubles;
each a remnant of something special.

I sit back, close my eyes –
not all the way –
absorbing beauty of radiant streams.
Dreams of seasons gone when all was whole,
nights silent with peace and love reign.

Tonight is different …
though special.
She is here, in my heart.
I do not weep, peace
formed by memories hung on a tree.

December 22, 2006

This is the second Christmas since Dorothy died, and tonight I am actually writing these words at the time of the experience. I am alone: my son lives in Alabama, my daughters near Minneapolis, and I must be here to be pastor at the candlelight service in a couple of hours. I have chosen to be alone this evening, wanting to write down my thoughts, wanting to spend time alone with my memories.

Dorothy's death has seemed to have taken the excitement out of life for me. I get along well, I think, but the special feelings tied to events are gone. Birthdays come and go, holidays pass by, important anniversaries are forgotten, and each day seems as though nothing special is happening. A certain monotone has set into my life, and highs and lows have disappeared.

I can't say I'm unhappy, certainly not depressed; however, I simply lack the excitement that used to be within me. Only time will tell if that special spark accompanying the holiday season will ever be rekindled. I rather doubt it will, but that is all right.

Tonight I will think about how she dressed on Christmas Eve, special meals with her, gift-giving; but I will especially remember holding her as we sat by the tree, wishing her a merry Christmas, and hearing the bells of Christmas ring in so many different ways.

Silent Bells of Christmas

Bells of Christmas ring out,
silent tolling falling on deaf ear.
All around me sounds of joyful singing,
laughter, happy greetings of "Merry Christmas."
How can swinging yuletide bells
make no sound?
Some part is missing.

The vibrations must be there;
seems everyone hears tones to which they move.
I sense nothing,
only sameness,
tonight the same as last,
so will be tomorrow,
time undifferentiated.

This eve I sit and contemplate
what is missing from the scene,
ponder memories, give thanks
for what I had.
All is quiet with a kind of peace,
but life has stolen
the sound from my Christmas bell.

December 24, 2006

I know I am not alone in my grief; time marches on for all of us, and none will be spared loss. For every couple there will come a time when one dies, and seldom does it happen that both should die at the same time. One product of my being alone is that I am much more aware of the losses experienced by others. Now when someone's spouse dies, I can rightfully say, "I know how you feel," but more importantly, I have resources I can recommend, personal wisdom I can share, and empathy I can provide. I find that people look for me, sometimes even seek me out, knowing that I have already walked the same stretch of life's road that they are only beginning. In a way, this is a healing process for me as well; because, I believe, it gives pur-pose for my life, and to some degree, an awareness of something good coming out of a very bad situation.

The Lutheran funeral service found in *Occasional Services: a companion to Lutheran Book of Worship,* includes these words: "Blessed be the God and Father of our Lord Jesus Christ, the source of all mercy and the God of all consolation. He comforts us in our sorrows so that we can comfort others in their sorrows with the consolation we ourselves have received from God."

Today, I attended the funeral for the wife of a person with whom I had taught school for nearly thirty years. In him I could recognize many of the same emotions I had felt, and I also could, probably quite accurately, predict what he would experience in the weeks and months ahead. I made him a promise I would be there for him, and he graciously asked for my company in the future.

Shared Pain

There is a funeral today
for one of a pair,
married fifty years or more.
He remains, she's gone;
I watch from a back pew.

We were there once,
my family and I,
sitting in the same place
her family now sits.
I know what they feel,
what they think is closure.
They are doing well – they think.

I know the day will come
when loss becomes too real,
spirits buckle,
panic opens its fierce maw,
heartache wells up inside.
He will need someone.
I've been there.
I'll be there.

December 30, 2006

I have walked my journey for one year and five months as of today. I suppose many think I should have gone further on my trek than I have; others, those who know, would say I'm right where I should be, wherever that is.

When I took my first steps, my knees buckled, literally, and I almost lost my ability to stand under the weight of the burden heaped onto my shoulders. This happened at the top of the stairs, going out of church as I followed her casket, being carried by six pallbearers. Only a very few people, those immediately behind me, saw what happened, and only one person ever said anything to me about my near collapse. As I analyze my journey thus far, I can't say that the burden has gotten one ounce lighter. Instead, I believe I have gotten stronger and am able to carry the load better – most of the time.

During the holidays, the load gets heavier, more noticeable. I assume this is true for most people over the days of Christmas, and that is a heavy time for my spirit. However, the most painful time for me, two years in a row now, has been New Year's Eve and Day. This puzzled me, because we never did much in the way of celebrating, but I think I have concluded why. I am a night person, becoming more alert and being most productive in the late evening, even up to midnight or so. Dorothy was a morning person, in bed by ten o'clock if she could be. And so, I would really have liked to have ushered in the New Year in grand style. She was content to greet it with a smile the next morning. I think I have a heavy heart on New Year's Eve, because I know I'll never celebrate with her as I would have liked.

All Dressed Up, But Nowhere to Go

I would have liked to have dressed up
in a tuxedo, wearing shiny shoes.
She would have polished her rings,
placed a strand of pearls around her neck,
worn a new gown: black to match her coat,
the elegant one with velvet cowl.
A gala celebration to attend,
good food, perhaps friends,
party favors to enjoy,
a silly hat, noise makers,
an excuse to act goofy.
We would have danced the night away,
toasted the New Year,
then danced more.

We never did,
usually asleep by midnight.
I would have liked to.

January 1, 2007

Perhaps one of the most difficult aspects of losing a loved one such as a spouse is the almost futile attempt to relate to others what it is like to be alone. Unless it has been experienced, and I'm sure others have felt this in non-grief situations, it is almost impossible to explain the experience of being in a crowd and still feeling totally alone.

I experienced this wherever I went: at baseball games, in a busy airport, and unfortunately, even with my family. This aloneness was something that for me did not go away, and like much of my new life, I simply learned to live with it and coped. Yet the aloneness didn't disappear. Wherever I go, whatever I do, half of me is missing, and I would not be surprised if I always feel this way.

It is no small thing to lose one's life partner.

Alone in a Crowded World

Airports are busy places
filled with blank faces
walking by my chair.
Thirty-six thousand announced,
the number in attendance at a game.
I cheer, eat junk food,
drink a Coke, cheer some more –
alone.

Church pews are filled; I take my place,
sing one note, alone.
Family gathering: daughters, son,
in-laws, grandchildren
laugh and talk. They don't see.
I hear, with no one.

Insulated in a crowd,
perceptions create senses
not known by others; alone
in a busy world.

January 13, 2007

I find that people misinterpret my attempts to express how I am when they ask, "How are you doing?" They seem to not be able to grasp the concept that there is a difference between doing well and being sad or lonely. Some do understand, but they are the ones who have walked this same journey, either with me or before me. They know the difference.

Even my children have little concept of how I feel, because they have not experienced being this alone, and so they have difficulty envisioning spending most of one's time in a house with no anticipation of there being anyone. It's one thing to be home alone and to be expecting your partner to join you at some time: an hour from now, a day from now, or even a week from now. This is unequivocally different, because the "sometime soon" has become "never," and that is a different kind of alone.

When a loved one dies, it is as though a large hole is punched through your soul, a hole that can never be completely filled.

A Dorothy-Shaped Hole

Time heals all wounds;
edges crust over, new tissue
forms in place of ragged borders.

Some holes gape too immense
to be filled;
craters remain to be felt by
exploring fingertips,
reminders of the loss of part.

My soul took a massive hit,
creating a pit of emptiness,
forever a reminder,
a Dorothy-shaped hole
nothing can fill.

Patch jobs fall short
of a permanent fix.
Blessings come in many forms –
daily I place my hand in the imprint

and sense the one it matches.

January 18, 2007

꒰ꏍ꒱

All we who grieve experience triggers: sounds, smells, sights that instantly jerk us into awareness of what our loved one had been. Our internal clock seems to be set for certain times and dates, and these can set off emotions that we have no idea exist, and strangest of all, the causes can be totally unknown to us. Then we might check the calendar and find that a date which had been important to the two is soon approaching.

The end of January is such a time for me, although I am well aware of what happened then, and I know that I am going to have some difficult moments simply because of the day on the calendar.

Dorothy's birthday was January 22, and we were married eight days later on January 30. My grief is deeper on those days than on most others, and I find that it is best to just let my grief happen. I don't try to keep a stiff upper lip or put on a good front for family or friends. Be honest, let it all hang out, and grieve as you will – no more, no less.

Nothing Special

January 22, a day on the calendar
to anyone who looks.
They can't see it stand out.
There's a large, dark border on
every new year's page. Can't you see?
It jumps out at me, why not you?

It must be special;
a friend walked with me
to where they bury people;
flowers were delivered today;
my son called to just say hi;
a favorite niece had an excuse for calling;
her mother wanted to share
a bit of news from home.

This morning I woke,
turned to an empty pillow,
needed to say "Happy Birthday."
January 22 – a day on the calendar.

January 22, 2007

Dorothy and I were married on my parents' wedding anniversary, January 30, and as undependable as was my memory, I never once forgot that day. It was always a special time for both of us, and even in the years when we had little money, we always celebrated by doing something special.

On our thirtieth anniversary, we had reservations at one of the fanciest restaurants in the area. Our grown family was with us, and I thought we would have a nice meal and then go home.

I had always said the only jewelry I would like would be a wedding ring with a diamond in it, never really intending to buy one. That night, after we had ordered our meal and before the food came, Dorothy took out a small box, opened it, and inside was a yellow gold wedding ring with three diamonds set in it. She started to say something, but immediately choked up as tears ran down her face. When she finally could, she said, "I had this nice speech ready, and now I can't say the words." Her tears spoke volumes, and I loved her so.

I thought, perhaps, I should place that ring on my right hand since I am no longer married, but the weight seemed to cause me to list in a direction I was not used to, and within an hour I had put it back on my left ring finger – where it belonged.

Home to Stay

Side by side, we sat at fancy table;
children watched in anticipation,
out came one small box marked
Bagley & Company.
She began to speak.
Words, choked off by spasms
wedged tightly in her throat,
drowned by tears, died.

Gripped firmly in velvet hands
a gold band, three diamond stars.
Silver band fell aside,
yellow slipped on third finger of left hand.
Joy flooded bright eyes.

It slipped off once,
moved to the other hand,
wouldn't stay,
migrated back home,
found a familiar groove,
restored balance to my being.
It hasn't moved since.

January 30, 2007

～

February has always been one of my favorite months. The icy grip of winter has begun to relax, the sun is getting higher in the sky, its rays feel warm on my back, and I have happy memories of family fun times in the out-of-doors. But perhaps the happiest memories are of finding a place where the afternoon sun was streaming through a window, lying down with Dorothy, and soaking up the sun's rays.

Now, when the sun comes in as it always did, I lie down, hold a pillow, and can almost feel her presence with me. It is still a special time.

Saturday Afternoon

Sun arcs across skies,
each day higher than the one before;
energy-packed rays strike retreating shoulders
with promising rays of February warmth.

It was time to hike frozen rivers,
sip hot chocolate under unmoving cataracts,
listen to gurgling water
slide beneath icy floor.

Time to open shades – wide –
lie on a sofa,
nap, hold tight
as two o'clock afternoon heat
surged over both.

Out daughters were born in early November.

February 3, 2007

Flowers were always a very important part of our lives, and now they are an even more important part of mine. I continued a tradition of forcing bulbs and other plants to bloom, long before their time was come. This year I bought bulbs for paper whites, narcissus, tulips, and hyacinth; subjected them to cold treatment, and then put them in trays filled with pebbles, added water, and within a few days saw green sprouts begin to emerge. Not long after, the plants were forced to bloom where they were planted.

In ways, we who grieve might be compared to those plants. We have no choice about the circumstances into which we are thrust. We certainly go through a cold period when our lives become frozen by the fear and panic of raw grief, and then we begin to thaw as the utter shock and despair begin to wane. It is then that we begin to bloom again.

No, we don't like where we're planted, and we would never choose to be where we're at, but bloom we do. Some who grieve find purpose in helping others, some in crafts and woodwork, some in sewing, some even write. There is no end to the different ways that people bloom where they are planted. The important thing is to allow yourself to grow, even though the place you are might not be the place of your choosing.

Forced to Grow

Tulip bulbs and hyacinth,
daffodils and paper whites,
are by nature planted in fall
to bloom in spring.
Kept in cold, some kinds
are placed in trays of pebbles,
vases filled with water,
unnatural, inhospitable places –
forced to bloom where they are planted.

Life, by nature, thrives on love
and warm embraces.
Forced into cold emptiness
by random acts of destruction,
survivor is planted in foreign circumstance.
Life goes on; roots form slowly.
We bloom where we are planted.

February 7, 2007

I dreamed last night, not of Dorothy, but of another. She had been a friend of mine since I was old enough to remember, and she grew up to be one of the most beautiful young women I'd ever seen. I could have loved her. She was way out of my league, though, high class in a class-conscious community. She faced a great deal of pressure to be popular, and her relationships were formed with older boys. We remained friends.

Three weeks before my first date with Dorothy, this "other one" and I, after meeting at a dance, went to Hibbing for a pizza. We talked and talked far into the night – about her boyfriend with whom she had just broken up. We remained friends. She never got back together with her boyfriend, had two failed marriages, and finally married a good man. It didn't matter, because I was happily married and had a family by that time. She was to me what the little red haired girl was to Charlie Brown, a.k.a., Charles Schultz.

But today, after dreaming of her last night, I could not get my mind off the what ifs.

She is alive today. She was really a good person who deserved more than what she got, at least in the beginning.

What if? I really didn't yearn for her, or regret in any way that things had gone the way they did; but I would have given anything to have been able to see her and to have her remember me and the night we had pizza in Hibbing – just to remind me I'm not forgotten by the world.

What If

❦

What if I were young again,
life stretching out before me?
What if I'd pursued another:
　　made the catch,
　　gotten caught?

What if I had chosen differently,
gone in another direction?
What if I had taken another turn,
become someone I don't know?
Would I be happy?

What if,
a futile thought of times not lived,
is best not pondered.

I think of what I would have missed:
children, warm bed, care,
devotion, quiet togetherness,
embraces, gentle touch.
What if I'd missed a special love?

February 8, 2007

When we are deep in grief, and even when we have begun to move on, there is an absolute tendency to withdraw into one's own being to escape the pain. The effort to get out of the house and do things is just that, an effort, and grieving souls tend to get so exhausted by the effort to move on that they begin to fold in on themselves. It can happen slowly, insidiously, this turning inward, so that one day you wake to find that life has begun to stand still.

I decided that I would purposely force myself to do new things, and I did. A large marathon, Grandma's Marathon, starts only a mile from my house, and I knew that housing for the runners was in short supply. I volunteered my guest room, and a couple from Houston, Texas, stayed the weekend with me. It was as though I had known them forever. I'll do it again next year.

I went on a mission trip to Talanga, Honduras, and I led small-group discussions following large-group lectures on theology. I now have friends in Talanga, and I am already planning for my next trip there.

Now these might not seem like appealing things for you to do – so don't, but find new and different things for yourself, activities that will get you out with new people and that will broaden your horizons. Then you will move forward instead of being eaten up by your grief.

Cast a Broad Shadow

Self folds in on self, swallowing life
until all focus is on loneliness.
Left to its own,
grief centers thoughts at the core of being,
convergence of personhood creates a capsule
of self-centered pity.
Life ends,

but,

life goes on.
Look outside self,
find those in need,
seek vistas not yet seen,
let personhood diverge from centered you.
Time to move from death to life.
Easy to say; difficult to do –
but DO!

February 14, 2007

I am not one who believes in mysticism, and I have not experienced visions, heard voices, nor does such mysticism fit my theology; although others might believe and experience differently than do I. That is why something that happened to me during my mission trip to Honduras surprised me so that I still have difficulty believing it happened.

The last morning, just before we left the rather primitive compound where we had stayed for ten days, we held a short worship service centered around Holy Communion. As I stood in that space, surrounded by mountains, Americans, Hondurans, and a pure blue sky, I felt Dorothy's presence so strongly it seemed she was there with me. Not only that, it was as though her spirit encompassed everything, spreading over the mountain ranges, over the compound, over me.

Naturally, such happenings cannot possibly be described with limited human vocabulary, and so it is impossible to come close to conveying what happened out there, but *something* happened. Whether it was of my own doing or something supernatural, I cannot possibly ascertain. All I know is that it happened at a time when Dorothy was far, far from my mind.

I must say that I sensed a deep feeling of approval for what I was doing, and a happiness for me that I cannot explain. I hope something similar happens again, but I know that such experiences are not to be conjured up.

Through a Mirror Dimly

There must be another world next door,
one we cannot freely enter,
separated from us by an opaque barrier.

A transparent window must exist,
one that opens briefly.
I looked through that window,
saw clearly what was lost.

Her presence was real,
warm and approving,
covering all I did, filling being
with peace and joy,
eyes with tears.

Glimpse lasted seconds,
an hour, a day, a week;
time stood still.
The window closed,
never willed to open.

Did it really happen;
was she present?
Perhaps there is a door
through which I'll one day pass,
stand beside her there.

March 11, 2007

On a beautiful day in March, as I walked with the sunshine warming my spirits, I couldn't help but marvel at where my journey had taken me. I remembered last year at this time; where I had been on this trail called grief, and I remembered the utter anguish I had been experiencing. I remembered that the full realization of my great loss had become reality and the over-whelming sense of alone had gripped me with its sharp talons. I remembered how I had felt a very real pain, not just an emotional pain, but a physical pain, as though my insides were being attacked.

Now, as I looked back, I began to make a mental list of what I had accomplished since Dorothy's death. Five poems had been published, and I had received a merit award in a contest. I had continued to serve my congregation as their pastor: had officiated at funerals, been involved with a couple of weddings, and preached over eighty sermons. I had written the better part of this book, and I had gone on a mission trip to Honduras. I had raised a garden: grown a large pumpkin patch that my grandchildren and the neighbor's grandchildren had pillaged before Halloween.

As my mental list of accomplishments grew, I couldn't help but be just a little pleased with myself, and at the same time, thankful for all of the opportunities with which I had been pre-sented. It was reassuring to know that life had gotten better, and that I was still living among the living, and was not dead.

Alive Among the Living

March, a delightful time of year:
buds on trees begin to swell,
crows engage in mating rituals,
images of garden plots grow in my mind.

I think I'll plant sunflowers in that corner –
she loved sunflowers; I'll remember her.
Will the strawberries sprout white blossoms
or did the harsh winter winds kill?
Raspberries will produce this year;
I can hardly wait!

A sense of loss remains;
scars do not disappear, only fade.
Raw, open wound healed over,
spot still tender to emotional touch.
I'm here; life goes on:
I live among the living.

March 22, 2007

One thing I know for certain: Dorothy's death has made me far more sensitive and compassionate toward those who are experiencing the same journey I have already walked. When I hear of someone whose husband or wife is dying, I know the anguish they feel; and I know that anguish will be followed by hope, whether real or manufactured on their part. I know the time will come when they'll be resolved to face the eventual outcome.

I also sense that some are willing to talk freely to me about their situation. I think, in most cases, I do the right thing. What most people need is not advice, not words of encouragement, not tears; they have enough of their own to shed. What most people need is a listener, someone who will listen to their story as many times as they need to tell it. And all they need in return is an acknowledgement that what they said was heard.

Listener

ॐ

"It is terminal, you know,"
he said;
eyes focused on a distant spot
of nothingness.
            I said I knew.
"She lost weight and couldn't stop,"
he offered;
jaw muscles bulged,
then relaxed.
            I said I guessed as much.
"You've been there, haven't you?"
he questioned;
shoulders sagged,
then stiffened.
            I said I had.
"Can we talk some more again?"
he asked;
eyes focused on a distant spot
of nothingness.
            I said I'd listen.

March 24, 2007

Dorothy and I found a special joy in wild birds. We fed them from several feeders in our yard, searched for them when we were on walks, listened to their evening songs together; but she was better at their identification than was I. She could even identify those rare birds that strayed out of their normal range.

Without a doubt, her favorite bird was the cardinal. Living in northern Minnesota, she seldom was able to enjoy seeing or hearing them when we were home; but whenever we visited places further south, she was always on the lookout for this red-bird.

Not all who grieve will find solace in a cardinal's song; but there will be other sights, sounds, or smells that will immediately trigger happy memories to restore the image of the one who is gone from your life. This is a gift we are given.

Red-bird's Song

Cardinal's love song
spills from pine tree top,
reaching hearing ears below,
glinting burst of sparkle
hidden from searching eyes.

She loved red-birds,
their iridescence more exciting
than any ruby-red gem;
song more welcome than a symphony.

I heard his call this morning;
was transported in memory
to a trail where we walked
hand in hand.

We heard his love song –
together.

March 31, 2007

The first Easter morning, eight months after Dorothy's death, I opened my eyes to the unbelievable cold of an empty tomb – at least that is what it felt like to me. I had to wake early, five o'clock in the morning, because I was the pastor who would conduct the sunrise service. The emptiness I felt was beyond description: we had, for our entire married life, believed in the promise of the day; and we rejoiced together, celebrating it with perhaps more joy than even Christmas. But this day was so different. It was as though I was in the empty tomb about which I would preach in only an hour or so. Unbelievably, I had been tapped to do four services that day, and the heaviness never lifted. By days end, I was still in the tomb, and I was exhausted.

This year – this year is so different. I awaken to the darkness, but with the belief and knowledge that the dawn will soon arrive; and I rejoice that I will see its manifestation. My life is different, undeniably different. I am not happy with the difference; but different is here, and there is nothing I can do to change reality. On the other hand, I can choose to embrace the different – and live.

I can only equate the new different to a resurrection: of my spirit, of my mind, of my life. A year *has* made a difference, and I have a life, new and different, but I have a life.

Resurrection Realized

My eyes open to an empty tomb;
blackness permeates my being,
suffocating nothingness fills my soul.
I am like one dead.

First hint of pink,
coniferous spires silhouette
against emerging light
as day begins its promise.
My soul stirs.

That stripped bare bursts to life:
white lilies,
songs of new creation fill the air,
promise of reunion fills my heart.
I live.

Resurrection of:
spirit, hope, the dead,
those drowned in sorrow;
my salvation draws near.
I *am* once more.
Blessed resurrection.

April 8, 2007

Ever since I was a child, I had been an avid outdoorsman; and during Dorothy's illness, I envisioned spending my days after her death hunting and fishing and allowing myself to be enveloped by the solitude.

Early last summer, I took my boat to a small lake, fished in placid waters, and even caught some fish. I thought, "This is good," and anticipated having a delicious fish dinner when I returned home. I cleaned the fish, cooked them the way I always did, and ate supper, but the meal didn't satisfy. Neither had the fishing trip.

As time has passed, I have learned that the old ways don't always fill me, and I have learned how much a part of my activities she was, including those activities she never shared with me. I learned that it wasn't necessarily the hunt or the fishing trip I enjoyed, but more so it was coming home to her, sharing my stories of what I had done and seen, and sharing a meal with her.

I don't know if I will ever regain my enthusiasm for hunting and fishing and camping, but it doesn't matter. I have new interests and new challenges ahead; and the future beckons me in other directions.

Hidden Hunger

A taut line taught a lesson:
life is different.
I caught two fish,
prepared and cooked them,
and ate.

Spirit hungered for her presence,
felt unsatisfied without dessert
of her approval.
The meal lacked spice.

Life changed:
fishing rod retires on wall,
creel an empty decoration.
Mission trips replace camping trips.
New life demands new living.

I hunger for her presence;
she would be proud of what I do.

April 18, 2007

There are some things we used to do together that were high on our list of priorities: walks in parks, attending church, working on our home, being with family, celebrating holidays; but if I had to choose one activity that we thoroughly enjoyed together, it would have been attending stage plays. We went to our first play in 1965, and that was the start of forty years of enjoyment. The last outing we had before Dorothy became too ill to go out anymore was to attend a staging of *Fiddler on the Roof.*

Since her death, there are many, many activities I don't do alone, or at all, but I have continued to attend plays. I go alone, and do not want others with me. I can be carried away to a fan-tasy world; and for some reason, I get comfort from sitting in a familiar seat, knowing if Dorothy were with me, she would be having a delightful time.

Coming back to reality can be difficult, but the trip is worth it.

On a Carousel

Enter a world called fantasy
where costumed actors
parade upon stage,
transport us to non-existent places.

We seldom missed a play
at our favorite house;
we would laugh and cry,
sometimes have biases and ideologies
jarred from their hiding places.

I attend alone – by choice;
am close to her there,
perhaps drawn into a jury room
filled with twelve frustrated men,

hold my sides because of laughter pain
when Princess Winnefred swims the moat;

can even be enticed to ride a *Carousel*.

It is a gift to live three hours
in a fantasy world,
to be carried away to a place
where death is make believe.

April 26, 2007

❧

A wonderful memory burst into my mind today, so real it was almost like reliving the past in live time. When we were somewhat newly married and had only one child, I coached track and field. On one particular day, a Friday, Dorothy had brought our daughter to the track, and they were sitting on a grassy bank across the field from where I was working. I looked across the expanse, and an image of perfection was burned into my mind, recorded forever somewhere in my brain cells.

My wife was wearing a yellow sport outfit, and my daughter had on a matching set, both hand-sewn by Dorothy. My daughter was only a toddler, but she was picking hands full of dandelions, and the two of them were braiding chains of flowers.

The details are as vivid today as they were thirty-eight years ago, and I am overjoyed that I have memories such as these. Without her in my life, could I ever have had such joy? The question is moot.

Movies on Demand

Blond-haired toddler frolics in dandelions,
picks bunches to make golden chains
for mother's hair.
Proud dad steals glances
across a field to admire wife, child –
day as perfect as it gets.
Movie loop plays on demand in mind,
screened on his memory.
A little sadness dims the scene
when credits run – she has star billing.
Living records memories,
no one escapes life's taping.
Reels catalogued somewhere in a brain,
run on demand to remind us of who we loved.
My matinee is of a perfect day.

May 1, 2007

Several years ago, I attended a workshop on death, dying, and grieving. It was conducted by an authority on grief who worked for a group of funeral homes, and I remember one of his statements that I believe showed a great deal of insight into the grieving process.

He related that often funeral directors would leave some small detail unattended. This was especially done in the case of the death of a child: a corner of a blanket in the coffin would purposely be left rumpled, or a piece of clothing left not quite right. I suppose there might be other small details not made perfect, but when the parents would see the imperfection, they would shake their heads a little, and then tuck in the blanket corner, or straighten the collar, or do whatever other small thing needed fixing. They didn't realize the gift they were being given – one last chance to do something for the one whom they loved so dearly.

Perhaps that is why we bring flowers to the grave, or sow fresh grass over bare spots, or make sure the headstone is straight. Perhaps it is a chance to do one last thing.

Readying for Memorial Day

A patch of grassless gravel
scars ground in front of polished granite.
Memory of her deserves better:
lush green carpet to soften footsteps,
flowers to freshen air with aroma,
perfuming gentle breezes.

He scrapes up useless grit,
pours out black nourishment from a bag,
rakes it level – sprinkles pieces of lawn
held in dry seed cases.
A grass mat will cover ugliness
of the day she was laid to rest.
An act performed for her.

May 6, 2007

Death leaves many walking in its shadow. Children who have lost a parent, even adult children, have a sense of something mis-sing in their lives, especially during various times of celebration. Dorothy and I had two daughters and a son, and I can only imagine their thoughts when Mother's Day is celebrated by those whose mothers are still living.

Each of my children has children, and I know that they become involved with their own families. My son makes sure his wife is honored on that day, and my daughters receive small gifts and cards from their children, but I also know their memories will turn to their own mother who meant so much to them. I'm sure the day is more than a little hollow.

She wasn't my mother, she was my wife; but I always remembered her on Mother's Day, always thanked her for the family she gave me, and praised her for the kind of mother she was to our children. I'll always be thankful to her for the gift she gave me.

Second Sunday in May

Small smiles shyly show
trepid anticipation.
Approval sought by searching eyes;
homemade gifts, cards,
offered by children to one who bore them.
Love manifest by hugs and kisses,
tears of happiness.

They have sons and daughters who
bring presents of their presence
to make hearts swell to breaking.
A pull, reaching back to Mom,
will enter thoughts today
in remembrance of who is missing
on *their* mother's day.

I too remember.

May 13, 2007

The gentle tones of our wind chimes drift through the air. Birds claim their territories with songs, and the first hummingbird of the season buzzes around looking for early flowers. I put out its feeder today.

All these bring back special memories: I bought her the wind chimes for a Christmas gift; the hummingbird feeder was bought by our son for her on a pleasant outing to a botanical garden. We would sit under our weeping willow and listen to the chimes, the birds' songs, and marvel at the hummingbirds' flight. Wonderful memories are all around me these days, and I welcome them, because they keep me connected to what we had and do not allow me to forget.

Tones of Peace

Winter freezes tones in place,
silence burrows deep into spirit,
smothering nature with nothingness;
deafening stillness blankets life.

Radiance of spring thaws sounds
that flow over earth:
Robin's call, frog's croak,
music to my ears.

Wind chimes,
hung where summer breezes
give voice to hollow pipes,
call me to peace and calm.

Red-glass feeder suspended near,
nourishes ruby-throated birds
who hum tones in harmony
to metallic intervals,
carry me in spirit
to a time and place we were.

May 30, 2007

W ith most books there comes a point where the reader turns the last page and finds "The End." Those words follow some sort of closure, a sad ending, a happy ending, a conclusion. Unfortunately, that is not going to happen. You see, the story of my journey has not ended, but it is at a point where each day, although it holds promise for me, is pretty much like the day before or like the day that will follow.

That is not to say that the days are all bad. They bring with them excitement sometimes, other times sadness, often some laughter – all the emotions that go with living. Even though, the specter of Dorothy's absence hangs over all I do; I miss her terribly. I don't think that I am the odd one when I say I expect I will always miss her; she was such an important part of my life for so long. She cannot be forgotten that easily, nor can her memory simply be put away out of sight.

I still view grief as a journey, and I picture a footpath disappearing to a vanishing point somewhere over the horizon. I don't know what is to be found at that vanishing point: will it be health, sickness, comfort, struggle? I do not know. If I were to write ahead and create an ending for this book, it would be pure fiction, because the future is unknown, and so we will part ways with one last poem that will provide a little closure, but not attempt to draw any conclusions about life in the next year, two years or eternity.

I know she waits there for me. When we will be reunited is not for me to know; but in the meantime, I will continue living, perhaps with a few tears, but always with a lifetime of memories.

Vanishing Point

A footpath weaves its weary way
through a worldly panorama,
wide at the place I stand,
narrow at distant horizon.
Lines in life picture
converge at a single locus
far from seeing eyes.
Blind to the future,
I follow where it leads.

We walked this path together;
she, shoved on ahead,
disappeared past the divide
that separates two worlds.

I'm left to navigate,
a stranger in a strange place,
as I move through unknown country
without chart or copilot.
Each new day moves closer
to *my* vanishing point.

I stumble along the way,
have in the past, will again –
I suppose;
each time picked up by friends,
even strangers. Or was it God?

The trail of living beckons;
its crookedness leads on.
Green pastures lie
near calm waters of peace.

I walk in the valley
of the shadow of a death;
evil does not frighten me,
it is defeated.
Comfort is mine
as I traverse this earth.

My Shepherd guides my steps
to a place where
the one I lost
will be waiting;
the feast-table is set –
just over the horizon,
where lives will meet again.

June 15, 2007

****

About the Author

꒜

Dennis Herschbach is a retired biology teacher who has served as a Synod Authorized Minister for the Evangelical Lutheran Church in America. He served a small congregation, Our Saviour's Lutheran Church, in Castle Danger, Minnesota, near the shore of Lake Superior; and lives just outside Two Harbors, Minnesota.

He is vice-president of the League of Minnesota Poets, and is also treasurer of Arrowhead Poets. Dennis has had work published in *Grief Notes*, *Lutheran Voices in Poetry*, and *Fire Ring Voices*, an anthology put out by Bemidji State University. His grief poems have been used by the St. Mary's Medical Center Grief Support Center in Duluth, Minnesota.

LaVergne, TN USA
20 January 2010
170592LV00002B/7/A